WHISPERS IN INK

POEMS ABOUT LOVE, SELF AND OTHER ATROCITIES

SUKRITI SINHA

To my parents, whose presence in my life has been the inspiration behind every verse in this collection. Your ability to love endlessly and yet be able to teach us tough love has infused these words with meaning and depth. With heartfelt gratitude, this book is dedicated to you.

Contents

Foreword   *vii*

Preface   *ix*

Acknowledgements   *xi*

Prologue   *xiii*

Poem

  1. Just One More Time -//   3

Poem

  2. दस्तक -//   7

Poem

  3. Help Me, And I Will Help You -//   13

Poem

  4. Fight -//   19

Poem

  5. Flower Buds -//   23

Poem

  6. Immortal -//   27

Poem

  7. तू ही तू -//   31

Poem

  8. All Of My Ugly - Might Just Be All Of My Pretty -//   35

Poem

  9. After -//   39

Abstract

  10. Your Strongest Pursuit -//   43

Contents

Poem

11. Life Goes On -// 47

Poem

12. Instinct -// 51

Abstract

13. Being Vulnerable Has Always Made Me Brave -// 55

Poem

14. हम -// 59

Poem

15. Joy -// 63

Note from the Author 67

Foreword

In this captivating collection of poems, Sukriti Sinha invites readers into a world where emotions find expression in the cadence of words.

With a keen sense of observation and a tender touch, the author crafts verses that resonate with the essence of the human experience.

As you embark on this poetic journey, prepare to be moved, inspired, and reminded of the beauty that resides in the simplest moments of life.

Preface

Welcome to Whispers In Ink!

These poems are my heart on paper, inspired by the simple moments of life. I hope you connect with the emotions woven into these verses and find a reflection of your own journey within these pages.

This book is my third time bringing life to paper, and I am forever grateful to each one of you that has picked up this book and helped make my dreams come true.

Enjoy the ride!

— Sukriti Sinha

Acknowledgements

In expressing my deepest appreciation, I want to acknowledge the incredible individuals who played pivotal roles in bringing Whispers In Ink to life.

To Maa, Papa and Didi, your unwavering belief in me and my words fueled my creative spirit. A heartfelt thank you to all my family, whose keen insights and meticulous work shaped these poems into their best versions.

I also extend my gratitude to my friends, whose contributions, whether large or small, added unique facets to this literary endeavor. This book is a collaborative achievement, and I am truly thankful for each person who played a part in its realization.

Lastly, to my readers, your constant support sustained me through the highs and lows of this creative journey. This book is as much yours as it is mine.

— Sukriti Sinha

Prologue

In this prologue, step into the threshold of Whispers In Ink.

These pages are a gateway to a world where emotions are painted with words. Join me in the exploration of love, loss, and the intricate dance of life.

The verses ahead are a glimpse into the tapestry of the human experience, inviting you to reflect, feel, and find resonance in the poetry that follows.

— *Sukriti Sinha*

Poem

just one more time.

1. just one more time -//

i almost say your name
when i'm asked to speak of myself.
you are my best friend;
now i have no one to tell
how i lost my best friend.
if stories were pieces of a person
then maybe our friendship
would breathe again,
because all i remember anymore
are stories about you and me
and i keep narrating them
hoping
that if i tell them enough number of times
then maybe i will mess up
and forget.
only,
i don't think
its working anymore;
your voice now narrates my thoughts.
i don't know if i should continue,
this is the only way i get to hear you again.
you were the lighthouse of my life,
now every glimmer

of every glimpse

seems like an achievement.

only,

i don't know whom to share it with.

you're my best friend. who do i tell it to?

Poem

दस्तक |

2. दस्तक -//

"tere jaane se toh kuch badla nahi. raat bhi aayi thi, aur
chaand bhi tha. haan magar ab neend nahi."
ek baat batana zara,
ehsaas kab hota hai
ki bas,
itni hi si thi humari kahaani?
kaise aata hai ye?
ant?
ek dhadaake ke saath?
ya kisi bacche ke qawwaali si dastak ke tarah?
aata bhi hai kya?
ya bas,
hum zabardasti kheench laate hai ise?
chaahe kahaani mein pyaar ho na ho,
ek ultimatum toh aata hi hai,
ek ant toh aata hi hai.
par jab tak vo ant dastak dete dete thak na jaati ho,
mujhe batao,
kya tum bhi wahi saari jagahon ka sair karte rehte ho?
kya tum bhi unn saari yaadon ke bal jeetein ho?
ek baat batana zara,
kya tum bhi uss kulfi ko baar baar chakh kar ye sochte ho ki
ab usme vo baat kyu nahi rahi jo pehle kabhi hua karti thi?

kya tum bhi bas unn hi saari yaadon,

unn hi saari paheliyon mein baar-baar baar-baar bas ghumte
rehte ho,

ulajhte rehte ho,

taaki bas ek aur baar vo ehsaas wapas aa jaaye?

vo sukoon, vo khushi, vo mithaas.

bas ek aur baad woh swaad mil jaaye?

ho sake toh mujhe batana matt,

magar kya tumhe yaad bhi hai vo mithaas?

vo ehsaas ki chaahe poori duniya khatam kyu na ho jaaye,

aakhir mein bas tumhara haath pakad ke baithna hi toh
matter karta hai.

tumhara vo meri haatho ke rekhaao ko pyaar se sehlaana,

aur mera tumhare haathon ko jhat se pakad lena.

ek baat batana zara,

ehsaas kab hota hai iss ant ke aane ka?

kya tum bas ek din mere manpasand gaane ko yuhi bina soche
samjhe gungunana band kar dete ho?

ya kya tum ye puchhna bhuul jaate ho ki mera din kaisa gaya?

ek baat batana zara,

ye ant bas dastak hi deti hai,

ya poora darwaza hi tod deti hai?

zara batana,

ye tod-taad mein halla hota hai,

ya bas khaamoshi hi sab khatam kar deti hai?

ek baat batana zara,

aaj jaane ki zid na karo toh gunguna bhi loge

lekin agar ruk bhi gayi toh thehraaoge kaise?
"tere bina zindagi se koi shikwa nahi
tere bina zindagi bhi lekin zindagi toh nahi"

Poem

help me, and i will help you.

3. help me, and i will help you -//

do not tell me
i am pretty,
if you haven't seen me slaughter
the sharks who wished to bite me.
do not tell me
i make a beautiful sound every time i speak,
if all you hear
is the rhythm of my cries for help,
the tone of my screams of anguish,
the melody of the cacophonies of my wrath.
do not tell me
you like the softness of my skin,
if you ignore the scars
of the tears that emerged
to relinquish the fire within.
outside.
everywhere.
do not tell me
i happen to charm you with my smile,
if you laugh at how you treat me yourself.
if you only like my smile,
my laugh,

if it's with you.
do not be offended by my jokes
if you're ashamed of your own truth.

instead,
tell me i am magnificent.
tell me you want to hold my sword
as i feed my sharks
that swim in the rivers of wisdom
leading us to the sea.
tell me i am resonant
tell me you will help me find my voice
even if it means
we lose our sense of pitch in the process
because you believe in our words
more than the melodies
you believe in our opinions
more than the people.
tell me i am warm
tell me you want to wrap me
around your arms
and for me to do the same
so we can shield each other from the volcano that lives inside
us.
tell me i have a ferocious laugh
tell me you want to make me smile triumphantly every day
to heal what you never scarred.

tell me

you don't think my scars need stars around them

in order to look presentable

tell me

i don't have to decorate my wounds

for you to accept them. to accept me.

tell me

you want to change your truth

and i will make every thing else

seem like a lie.

Poem

fight.

4. fight -//

how do i barge at you when all i have ever known is to escape?
"how do i throw a punch when i've always just been focused
on dodging the blow"?
they ask me to fight back every time i see you coming
and i ask them why should i worry about you coming in the
first place?
how do i separate myself and face the person that i am,
rather than what i should have been?
i have forgotten how to introduce myself.
please help me not forget how to be.

Poem

flower buds.

5. flower buds -//

time and again,
i try to write you a poem.
broken words,
broken sentences,
an unbreakable will to continue to choose you
every single day,
every single moment,
an unbreakable will to keep loving you,
more every single day,
every single moment.
i fall short of words;
they fall out of my heart
and then fall into the pit in my stomach
that you keep filling with flower buds
every time i see you smile.
i tell you i do not have words to describe this feeling
that overwhelms me every time i meet your eyes
and just hearing that puts a smile on your face,
and just like that i do not quite remember what being alone
really felt like
because you've filled the pit in my stomach
with flower buds
that you keep watering

every single day,
every single moment.

Poem

immortal.

6. immortal -//

now,
if defeating the writer inside me
brings you even an ounce of happiness,
i will burn all my ink for you.
i will value you more than i value my pages
if that means this love(¿) immortalises
like my poems about you.
i've known words all my life
i hope to know you just a little longer.
it is difficult to not notice
how beautiful
your heart is,
and it is impossible to not notice
how beautiful
you make the world to be.

Poem

तू ही तू।

7. तू ही तू -//

shikayat karu bhi toh kisse?

raahat bhi toh tujhse hi milti hai.

kyu jaane ki zidd kar baitha hai?

laut ke bhi toh yahi aana hai.

kuch shikayatein, kuch duwaaein,

sab tere naam.

har pal mohabbat karti rahi mai tujhse

par jab rab hisaab maangega,

toh kar dungi shikayat mai bhi

ki aakhri ke do pal kam the.

thori baatein tu kare, thori mai karu,

baaki khamoshiyan kar lengi.

titli si udaan udne lagi hu mai,

jo jugnu sa roshni dene laga hai tu.

shikayat karu bhi toh kisse?

har takleef ka hal bhi toh tu hi nikaalta hai.

kyu jaane ki zidd kar baitha hai?

tujhe tujhse hi paana baaki hai mera.

kyu jaane ki zidd kar baitha hai?

itne jaldi tujhe yaad karne ki

kaabiliyat nahi hai mujhme.

saath chahiye tera,

yaadein banane ka mauka toh de.

Poem

all of my ugly – might just be all of my pretty.

8. all of my ugly - might just be all of my pretty -//

my tongue works faster than my brain does
and maybe that is why
i have only ever loved
after already having tasted the wounds;
only ever regretted
after having devoured the stars.
i forget what it was
i wish i never forget what i felt.
i own the wounds i own the stars
i caused it all.
is changing the same as evolving?
is evolving the same as growing up?
i am taller now. smaller, still.
i forget what it was,
i hope i never forget how it felt.
i do not know how to keep my pretty away from my ugly,
it is all me.
we're all the same.

Poem

after.

9. after -//

i am made of memories i can't seem to remember.
i write the poetry i cannot live;
i live the poetry i cannot write.
i kill everything in between,
i live by what comes after.
i am made of memories i am begging to forget.

Abstract

your strongest pursuit.

10. your strongest pursuit -//

maybe one day you will relate to the poems about being in love and being loved back, and be indifferent to the ones about longing for it like it's something distant and unattainable.

maybe one day you'll realise that you are worthy of all the love you give out even when there's no one in sight, of all the love you wish you got even when everyone's around.

maybe one day you wouldn't have to think twice before holding hands with your partner, before hugging your friend, before smiling with your teeth wide open.

maybe one day you will realise there are people out there who notice when you're a bit too quiet, who notice when your lips quiver with excitement.

one day, you will realise that every ounce of love that you've ever given out is coming back to you.

one day, you will realise that you should never have to feel that maybe you should not care so loudly. one day, people will be so soft and careful with your heart, you will wonder why you ever thought of silencing it.

one day, you will realise that loving has always been your strongest pursuit.

one day, the nurturer will get nurtured.

one day you will not be embarrassed to show your wanting.

one day you will indeed reap what you sow, perhaps more.

Poem

life goes on.

11. life goes on -//

will i be something?
am i something?
you already are.
you always were.
and you still have all the time in the world to be.
the world never stops; life must go on.
is that always such a bad thing?
life will still go on
if you do not have a jumpstart.
life will still go on
if you sit and breathe for a while
and see the world in a grain of sand
and hold eternity in the palm of your hands.
life will still go on
if you smile a little longer,
if you love a little too fiercely.
life will still go on
if your heart breaks,
life will still go on
when you have to grieve.
love is never lost. life is never wasted.
life will still go on,
it is seldom a bad thing.

Poem

instinct.

12. instinct -//

i burn and i crumble
yet i am perfectly still.
whose peace am i preserving?
i wait and i wait and i wait
until my rage eats me up from the inside.
the instinct to shield oneself
in the protection of the oppressor
will always be present
in a system built upon the bones
of the marginalised.
where do i keep my body
and how do i cope inside of it
if my bones keep shattering and crumbling
and yet all i can do is sit still
and wait and wait and wait some more
and stomach it all in as i burn.
i wish i could burn the oppression along.
my anger is nothing
but my life's attempt
to gain a little bit of dignity
over the cruel joke
of the shattering shame of loneliness.

do you understand
how much violence it took
to be this gentle?

Abstract

being vulnerable has always made me brave.

13. being vulnerable has always made me brave -//

"you love too much, you trust too soon."

"why do you say that like it is supposed to be a bad thing?"

"how is it not?"

"i would much rather get hurt than not be the reason someone feels loved and belonged."

"what good is that if walking with them entitles them to walk all over you?"

"sometimes. other times, they will carry you on their backs all the way. being vulnerable has always made me feel brave, telling people i care about them has always made me infinitely more strong."

"what do i when i am stuck being the one who always loves more?"

"congratulate yourself."

Poem

हम |

14. हम -//

"aa chal ke tujhe mai leke chalu ek aise gagan ke tale, jaha

gham bhi na ho, aasu bhi na ho, bas pyaar hi pyaar rahe."

kayi dino se

apni kahani likhne ki koshish kar rahi hu

agar ho sake,

toh humari kahani ki shuruat kare?

kayi dino se

tumhare baare mein kuch likhne ka soch rahi hu

agar ho sake,

toh batana aakhir shuruat karu bhi toh kaha se?

kavita likhne ke pehle na jaane kitne sawaal mann mein aaye

likhu? ya tum fir kuch keh kar hass doge?

ek kavita mein itna kuch batana mumkin bhi hai?

hindi mein likhu ya angrezi mein?

fir yaad aaya

ki jo bhi kahu, jis bhi bhaasha mein likhu

tum toh yuhi sun ke muskura doge

"ho akhiyan kare ji hazuri, maange hai teri manzuri

kajra siyahi din rang jaaye, teri kasturi rain jagaye"

ha,

bhale hi beech beech mein tok ke tum kisi shabd ka arth

puchhne lagoge

aur mai jhat se tumhari naadaani pe hass baithungi

ya kisi line ko padh ke khud hi aise hass doge ki mai hi sharma
jaau
accha batao
kis baare mein likhu?
kaise chunu ki sabse acchi cheez kya lagti hai mujhe tumhare
baare mein?
batao, kaunsi cheez hai tumhare baare mein jise mai shabdo
mein laake humesha ke liye amar na kar du?
samay ke tarah hai humari kahaani
shuruaat kab hui iska koi anumaan nahi hai
aur kahani ka ant kab hoga ye pata nahi
par tab tak ke liye bas humare shabdo se amar ho jaaye yahi
chaahti hu
"tu jo mujhe aa mila, sapne hue sarphire
haathon mein aate nahi, udte hai lamhein mere
meri hasi tujhse, meri khushi tujhse
tujhe khabar kya be-kadar"

Poem

joy.

15. joy -//

i don't want to miss anymore.
i do not want to go about all my life
just searching for the joy
i so effortlessly felt as a child.
there is joy around all the time.
i don't want to miss out anymore.
you miss out by focusing on missing out. there is joy all around,
but i am the source.
there is love in my friendships;
and there is love in creating art.
there is love in nodding along to a child's babbles;
and there is love in buying your friend popcorn while waiting for them at the station because you know your friend will smile at the sight of it.
there is love in picking out flowers for your mom;
and there is love in making sudoku puzzles for your best friend because you know it'll help her believe she can achieve all she wants.
there is love in purposely losing a game of chess;
and there is love in buying your partner a little something every time you go out shopping.

there is love in texting on the dead group-chat to remind your classmates about a forgotten memory;
and there is love in going all the way to your best friend's house when her favourite celebrity couple broke up or when she lost her guitar pick.
there is love in smiling at a stranger;
and there is love in walking miles to get your neighbour a cake that he mentioned he liked months ago when you know he won't celebrate his own birthday.
there is love in keeping aside the rotten tomatoes at the grocery store so that others don't buy the wrong ones either;
and there is joy in staying up all night dancing away with your cousin when you promised to help them study.
there is love in buying biscuits for a dog on the street;
and there is love in not wanting to bother your friends about your inconveniences.
there is love in high-fiving a kid;
and there is love in recording and singing songs over video call for your friend who lives in a different country.
there is love.
there is love all around that is just waiting to be seen
but is it really so important
for it to be noticed by not just you yourself?
all my love comes from me
and what is love if not the ultimate joy?
there is joy all around,
but i am the source.

joy isn't something that happens to me,
it is always within me.

Note From The Author

In closing Whispers In Ink, I extend my sincere gratitude to those who embarked on this poetic journey with me. Thank you for lending your time and emotions to these verses.

As you reach the end, may these words linger and resonate in the corridors of your thoughts. Until our paths cross again in the pages of another story or poem, thank you for sharing this chapter with me.

For any reviews, suggestions or constructive criticism, please write an email to sukriti265@gmail.com or send a text to @sukritiiiii_ on Instagram!

—*Sukriti Sinha*